Oliver's Adventure
Skiing at Mount Snow

By Michelle Puzzo • Illustrated by Christen Pratt

green
writers
press

Giving Voice to Writers & Artists Who Will Make the World a Better Place
Green Writers Press | Brattleboro, Vermont
www.greenwriterspress.com

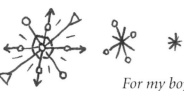

For my boys, I dreamed of you for so long, I love you with all my heart.
Mommy.

~

ISBN: 978-0-9994995-0-4

Published in United States by Green Writers Press.
Visit us on the web @ www.greenwriterspress.com or call 802-380-1121.
DISTRIBUTED BY MIDPOINT TRADE BOOKS, NYC. ORDER@MIDPOINTTRADE.COM

Visit Mount Snow @ www.Mountsnow.com or call 800-889-4411
for ski school and childcare information.

Visit www.moover.com or call 802-464-8487.

Visit www.wafflecabin.com to find a location near you.

Portion of proceeds to be donated to Stepping Stones for Stella,
a nonprofit organization founded by Oliver's cousin which
helps to produce all-terrain buggies for children with
disabilities to be able to experience being at the beach
or the snow. Visit www.steppingstonesforstella.org
for more information.

PRINTED ON PAPER WITH PULP THAT COMES FROM FSC-CERTIFIED FORESTS, MANAGED FORESTS THAT GUARANTEE RESPONSIBLE ENVIRONMENTAL, SOCIAL, AND ECONOMIC PRACTICES BY LIGHTNING SOURCE. ALL WOOD PRODUCT COMPONENTS USED IN BLACK & WHITE, STANDARD COLOR, OR SELECT COLOR PAPERBACK BOOKS, UTILIZING EITHER CREAM OR WHITE BOOKBLOCK PAPER, THAT ARE MANUFACTURED IN THE LAVERGNE, TENNESSEE PRODUCTION CENTER ARE SUSTAINABLE FORESTRY INITIATIVE® (SFI®) CERTIFIED SOURCING.

..... off to the slopes!

Can you
arrange the letters
to spell Oliver's
name?

_____

- - - - - - - - - - - - -

_____

_____

- - - - - - - - - - - - -

_____

The Moover is a
<u>BUS.</u>
How is it different
than a school bus?
How is it the
same?

We ride the Moover to Mount Snow, a ski
mountain in Vermont.

A chairlift
is what we ride to
the top of the mountain.
How many do you
see on
Bluebird Express?

Dad takes me to Snow Camp.
He is an early bird for Bluebird.

Do you
know what
"Bubbly"
means?
What makes you Bubbly?

After Ski School Dad promised me that we could look for the Golden Bubble that makes me so bubbly!

Can you
count how many items
Oliver has
to put on before
he goes in the snow?

Before I got on the bus my parents helped me put on all my gear. My gear keeps me safe and warm.

Thermals

Goggles

Snowpants

Helmet

Neck Warmer

Gloves

Do you like to
play in the snow?

What do you like to
do in the
snow?

My mom is dropping my little brother off at Cub Camp, where he will play with his friends.

How many
snowflakes
do you see?

18

My ski teacher is called a ski instructor.
He teaches me how to put on my ski equipment.

Skis

Ski
Boots

Poles

Ski
Instructor

What shape is
a bubble?

How many do you
see?

It's so important to stay in our "bubble." We don't want to ski into our friends.

What is the
difference
between skiing
and snowboarding?

On the ski trail, heading down the slopes,
I see Stevie snowboarding.

Can you find the
Black Diamond?
It is the hardest
trail to ski down!

I saw Mom having a lesson at Tumbleweed, that's a Green Trail.

Falling can be fun!
How is Oliver's
Mom feeling
after she fell?

She told me she fell, but got right back up. Falling is fun!

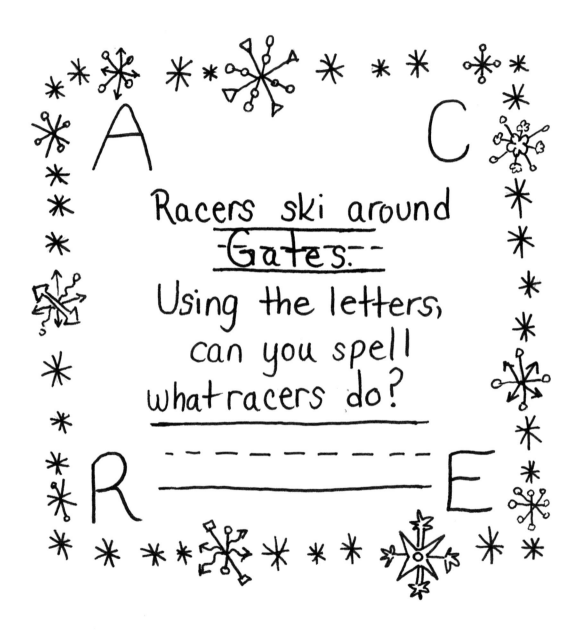

A   C

Racers ski around
__Gates.__
Using the letters,
can you spell
what racers do?

R   E

I see people racing. I hope one day I can be on the Race Team at the Training Center.

How long does it
take to go tubing?

5   10   30
      seconds?

Mom said she was meeting Dad at Cuzzin's for lunch, and after school we will go tubing.

What shape is a
Waffle?

Brother and I asked to make a quick stop at Waffle . Cabin.

What colors
do you see
in the
fire?

After tubing we were tired. We went into the lodge to sit by the fire.

Have you ever
had a dream?
What do you
dream of?

That night I had dreams of how to make. "french fries", "pizza wedge" and doing. tricks.

About the Author

MICHELLE PUZZO was born in Connecticut and graduated from the University of Connecticut in 1998 with her BS in Physical Therapy. She exhausted all options to have children, due to infertility, and she had her first son, Oliver, via surrogacy in 2012 and her second son, Finnigan, was born via surrogacy by the same gestational carrier, in 2014. She bought a condo at Mount Snow in 2012, and fell in love with Vermont. Her son Oliver began ski school and she was inspired to write her first children's book based loosely on his experiences and for her desire to teach people about what an amazing experience kids and families have at Mount Snow. Oliver quickly outskied her so more lessons are scheduled for this season. She is currently working on her next book.

Oliver (left) and Finnigan.

About the Illustrator

CHRISTEN PRATT has a B.S. in Art Education from Central Connecticut State University and is an elementary art teacher at a magnet school in central Connecticut. Christen is an active artist, a mother of one vibrant little girl, and Oliver's art teacher! She and her daughter share a love of the outdoors, including playing in the snow and traveling to Vermont. Christen looks forward to teaching her daughter to ski! With a background in culinary arts, as well as fine arts, Christen thrives in many creative facets and is passionate about teaching, spreading creativity, and family.

CPSIA information can be obtained
at www.ICGtesting.com
Printed in the USA
LVRC022102181218
600951LV00001B/6